POTENTIAL

Lush's Hierarchy of
Digital Transformation

POTENTIAL

Lush's Hierarchy of
Digital Transformation

"a prescription for cloud platform value"

Greg Lush

LMWS | 2019

LMWS books may be purchased for educational, business, or sales promotional use. For information, please email: greglush@lastmileworkersolutions.com

ISBN: 978-0-359-82807-4

FIRST EDITION: 2019

Last Mile Worker Solutions, LLC.
31 Promontory
Dove Canyon, CA, 92679

www.lastmileworkersolutions.com

Dedicated to...

those unafraid to travel past the horizon and discover that the digital world is far from flat

Contents

Acknowledgements

To all the individuals and organizations which have influenced my perspectives over the years, a huge thanks. I am speaking to you; those thoughtful leaders, managers, and workers who are struggling with, and committed to helping your organization digitally evolve. Each chapter and section are designed to sparks ideas and give you the confidence to challenge conventional thought. To evolve we must disturb the present in order to obtain a brighter future. The cloud is here to stay, just look up!

Foreword

By Greg Lush

Most individuals in today's enterprises may only use a few pieces of technology; a transactional system (CRM, accounting, work order management), a communication system (typically email and/or a messaging service), Microsoft Office (Word, Excel, PowerPoint), and possibly a special purpose application (AutoCAD, etc.). While I have my "broad stroke paintbrush" in hand; I would bet that most people are using a small percentage of the functionality provided within any of these tools.

I must be honest with you, this has and continues to bug the crap out of me. To pile on to that frustration, licensing models have also changed over the last few years from a capital (purchase the software) to an expense (where you just rent the software ... forever). If you have not already been asked, or woke up and realized; am I really paying all that money for just email and file storage? Ouch. And so our journey begins: finding a way to extract greater value from our digital assets.

Over the last several years I have been experimenting and testing different approaches to help folks and I do believe that a prescription exists. This will be one of a series of sections, building upon one another, to lead you and your organization to the land of complete digital adoption. Forget that! The land of transformation where adoption is just a pebble in the rear-view mirror. This book is dedicated to those unafraid to travel past the horizon and discover that the digital world is far from flat.

Think about the amount of change which has occurred over the last three decades with business technology. Not just in the tools themselves, but the change in the IT professional has also been quite dramatic. I suppose how this change has been accepted (or not) may be an illustration of how much you believe in the pigeon theory. Long ago, while with a fellow worker who was complaining about constant change, he shared with me the "Pigeon Theory." Picture that you are a pigeon standing on a rooftop and, suddenly, a cat appears just five feet from your current position. You can feel the presence of the cat but refuse to turn your head, instead using your quietest internal voice to repeat, "the cat is not hungry, the cat is not hungry." Our business computing environments have and will continue to change, regardless of your ability to adapt and see what is right before your eyes.

The real value of technology is generated by true adoption, as opposed to the multi-decade approach of implementation and deployment. Unfortunately, many of the technology professionals working within organizations struggle to change lanes, transitioning from the bytes to the people. An entirely different approach is required, and this is the motivation behind assembling this prescriptive series on my hierarchy of digital transformation. Without changing our approach, I fear that organizations will be content with simply moving workloads like e-mail and files to the cloud, failing to unlock the tools which can truly transform an organization.

Influenced by experimentation over the last few decades, I have assembled a four-step approach to succeeding in cloud platform adoption focused on extracting business value. This book will provide tactical approaches which influence behavior. If you have read any of my prior blog posts, you will discover that leveraging the Microsoft stack has been a part of much of my career. That said, the advice and insights discussed are technology agnostic; this is all about transformation and thus your employees, customers, and partners take center stage.

Like Maslow's theory, I believe that a funnel exists compelling all to start at the bottom and work their way to the top. Realizing the full potential of your cloud platform requires you to travel through four stages, they are:

1. Digital **reputation** | defined as; available, consistent, and trustworthy. Once established digital habits will be formed.

2. **Contextual** computing | digital collateral without context to a customer, site, work discipline, is simply noise.

3. Shared **insights** | collaboration creates 1+1=7 results; exponentially enhancing internal and external value.

4. Predicting **outcomes** |differentiation, in any market, comes from producing unexpected perspectives which positively alter your course.

Now that we've set the stage, go ahead and start the book and leverage the strategies and tactics used in practice today, designed to help future proof your businesses in the Digital Age. The first chapter will unpack the meaning and steps you may take to build a solid Digital Reputation.

Digital Reputation

I promised to follow up with some tactical steps to help future proof your business in the Digital Age, and the first step is building and protecting your digital reputation. I know – digital reputation, you are kidding me, right? You might be thinking, all that I have ever needed is the ability to send and receive email. Maybe occasionally, store a file or two. Are you saying to yourself; I am totally on board – look, I have moved my email and file management tools into the cloud; I am the symbol of progress!

Is it possible those words are rattling around in your head? My guess is that you may also be the person who finds themselves perpetually buried in their inbox, wondering if things will ever change. I would say you're not alone.

We've now reached a tipping point where cloud-based tools are agile and affordable, allowing us all to consider transforming our businesses for the digital age. However, this endeavor fundamentally modifies how we look at these tools. While systems still need to be implemented and deployed, the time in these development phases will be brief. Instead, your efforts will need to be focused squarely on adoption, a discipline often discussed and filled with mediocre performance and excuses. An example I've heard: "This is a cultural and training issue, it has nothing to do with the technology." While the sentence may be correct, it is one of the core reasons why adoption seems to be limited to a "checkbox" for many of our strategies.

I speak from decades of experience as a Chief Information Officer, our ability to transform organizations into doing business differently was generally isolated at best. Now, decades later, I still struggle with the point of it all. I feel like a dog with a bone in that I just cannot shake the challenge of getting everyone, not just early adopters and innovators, headed in the same direction. The trick has always been leveraging applications which are perceived as noncompulsory (aka valuable applications), and inspiring people to see past their perceived assumptions of applicability. Through recent experiences deploying cloud platforms, this hierarchy of digital adoption has been put to the test across a variety of business sizes. Proven time and time again, if you follow this hierarchy, succeeding at the first step before proceeding to the next, you will holistically transform your organization today, while making it future proof for tomorrow.

The Key to Your Digital Reputation Is Building Trust

So, what exactly am I referring to when I talk about a solid digital reputation? To start, I would ask you to think about a person that you know who has an excellent reputation. My guess is that your list would include characteristics such as trustworthy, reliable, helpful, and accessible. A relationship cannot advance without these behaviors; the same applies to your adoption aspirations. It is not uncommon for folks to believe the reason they subscribed to a well-known cloud platform was due to their reputation as a provider. Unfortunately, while that is important, you are miles from having your users comfortable with their new operating environment. Without a strong digital reputation, each of the subsequent digital adoption steps will become exponentially more difficult.

We all know that change management is a team sport and building or fortifying your digital reputation is no different. The only path to achieving your adoption goals is to establish trust and a sense of purpose. Generally, the applications deployed within the first phase of the hierarchy of digital transformation should be a relatively straightforward and low friction applications to deploy, such as email. However, don't get fooled by the adoption rates on this transactional system. Like Maslow's theory, other than getting the environment "stood up," satisfying the groups "physical needs" is nothing to write home about.

If you remotely believe that our digital world is not flat, I encourage you to forge on for a better understanding of the digital hierarchy. We will build on elevating your digital reputation and allow you to proceed through the hierarchy of digital transformation, next discussing what to do when you are crippled by choice.

Avoid being crippled by choice

During winter you often hear people say, I can't wait for the warm weather; in the summer just the opposite, it's too hot! Business systems are similar — years ago we wanted to have more choices and the freedom to choose our own path. Now, our trouble is that we have so many options it can be downright overwhelming. At first glance, our concerns are not getting locked in as with monolithic systems of yesteryear. Instead we try to find a platform which serves our needs today with an eye towards the future. When contemplating the selection of a cloud platform, people fall into two camps: cardigans and cobblers.

- **Cardigans** represent "the establishment." Just five years ago I would have agreed that placing yourself in this community meant significant compromise. Giving in to "the man" with the largest organizations. However, today, as transactional and valuable (referring to all other software, personal productivity, artificial intelligence, IoT, etc.) tools get more degrees of separation, your accounting system does not have to dictate the other value packed tools within your business.

- **Cobblers** are defined as those constantly seeking software, which appears low cost on the front end yet has no continuity between applications. A few years back I gave some credence to those in this community. Ready at any cost to fling the bird at the man, just because they are frightened to lose their station as the "go-to person." Cobblers yearn for the glory days when the organization was held completely captive by their almost magical talents

Keep in mind that the selection of a platform has one ounce of technology and nine ounces of people. You must understand your demographic and plan accordingly. Having a split camp will be exponentially more challenging, thus your first task is to get everyone singing, or at least humming, from the same hymnal.

Now that you are harmonizing fantastically, it is time to peel this onion back a bit and get into some details. When selecting a platform, to run your valuable applications, you may consider some of these elements. I like to make decisions and communicate change as objectively as possible, so assigning value numbers to each of the elements is advised. Although your list may vary, these will get you on the right track to making an informed and deliberate decision regarding your valuable platform selection(s):

- **Availability**. Without question, your environment needs to be available 24 hours a day, 365 days a year. Listen with an open mind — as security has changed with cloud, offerings often do not require sophisticated VPN connections.

- **Compliance**. Legal and HR must be involved in this element. I encourage you to consider that most of your cloud platform partners will be dealing with similar challenges. Don't hesitate to ask how your partner is addressing common issues. So often we see an uninformed legal or IT security organization strangle any potential of innovation as the result of thinking "this is how it always used to work." Also, get comfortable around compliance issues which may be your concern within the next handful of years, a notable example is the general data protection regulations (GDPR).

- **Encryption**. Our ability to pass a key, issued by the publisher and passed to the consumer, has been protecting information for years. Depending upon your industry, and in many cases your customers' requirements, encryption strategies will vary significantly. Choose an organization which has a positive track record of encryption with their keys and allows you to manage and control your own encryption keys if so desired.

- **User Experience**. My expectation in today's day and age is that I will be able to digitally "pick up where I left off" from any device, anywhere and the tools will be the same. The way in which I interact will not be impacted by the size of my screen, which is much easier said than done. If in your selection process users are expected to understand different user interfaces and experiences from application to application, get ready for a steep adoption climb.

- **Integration**. Very commonplace within transactional-based systems (accounting, HR, work order management, purchasing, etc.) and becoming more mainstream with valuable applications as well. Graphing is the new term and process, an evolution of a services-oriented architecture (SOA). Set your sights high as your ability to leverage features across valuable applications is becoming the ante to participate in the cloud platform game.

- **Master data**. A perfect computing environment, regardless of the variety of applications, will always have one version of the truth. One account record, one contact, and one place to go for the latest insights. As with many things over time, cost and availability become more of a reality for the masses. The trick is not placing or enforcing the data to be stored in one location but instead the convenience of leveraging this single bit of data in multiple applications. You must demand this functionality within your cloud platform.

- **Partners**. The ecosystem of partners surrounding any cloud platform is important especially if you plan on extending the out-of-the-box functionality. Today, those jumping straight into customizing systems have not taken the time to really learn their platforms. In 2019, except for highly regulated industries, those choosing customization over configuration are often driven by their egos or attempts to make themselves irreplaceable (shame, shame).

- **Visualization**. Your platform, out-of-the-box, must have a vehicle for you to visualize the information, period. These visualization tools, commonly known as dashboards and reports, shouldn't just be created as "eye candy." Rather, these tools must derive action, allowing people to visualize their business in a unique way. Avoid the consideration of tools which make your users a slave to the data, turn it around and make sure your visualizations can help users manage by exception instead.

These elements, when weighted and scored by those within your organization, will provide direction and support for your cloud platform selection and help you from being paralyzed by the wide range of options you have.

Driving adoption of Valuable apps

There is no doubt that, in the business world, not all software applications are created equal. Take for instance your transactional systems, email, accounting, etc. These applications are designed, configured (sometimes customized), implemented, and deployed. Notice that adopted was not once mentioned. Transactional applications, or anything that is repeated with limited user-choices, once trained is quickly institutionalized.

On the other hand, when you look at valuable applications, all the other software which is not transactional, the path to success is a bit different. All the steps discussed for the transactional system are the same with the addition of adoption at the end of the cycle. Some equate transactional systems to those required by the business, while the valuable applications are left as optional. And so, the struggle begins with prioritizing these valuable applications and inspiring your colleagues to leverage their power.

Many schools of thought exist regarding how change occurs within an organization. Depending upon the company a top-down approach, grass roots movement, or frankly a combination of both will lead to success. There is one thing in common regardless of change management style: people need to believe in the mission. Belief is a tricky thing, you must have credibility and the trust of your community. Yet, it goes much deeper than that and falls back to that simple adage, "lead by example." While many would agree that you yourself must be a practitioner, it is not always that simple. Imagine for a moment that you are a branch manager responsible for hundreds of employees and tens of thousands in annual revenue. Now you are presented with this vast landscape of a cloud platform. Down deep inside you know this is the direction you must travel; however, running a business and learning a new toolset is a tall order. Thus, like many things we reprioritize those which are the foggiest from our perspectives and hesitate to socialize these tools with any zeal. Not to mention, have you seen the breadth of most of the cloud platform offerings? A lot of choices and too many possibilities.

Deployment Vs. Adoption

So, we come back to that idea of deployment or adoption. If you are hell-bent on maintaining your approach as you did with transactional systems, save yourself some time and don't worry about all the other cloud platform possibilities. Yet if you have gotten this far my guess is your interest is to see what's beyond that digital horizon. I strongly believe that adoption is 80 percent resolve. Depending upon the individual, they may resolve to use a valuable application immediately or wait for others to go first, and both are totally acceptable. Your mission, if you accept it, is to get everyone to their "aha" moment as quickly as possible. Once individuals "get it" you will be amazed at how much faster your adoption efforts proceed. One of the tools that we have used to help reduce anxiety, as the result of the unknown, is named a transformation cycle.

Transformation cycles are loosely defined as a visualization of a business's progress from the introduction of a *valuable* application to that software solution reaching the "plateau productivity." This single page diagram is highly effective as it allows the organization's leadership to dictate the path and visually see its progress. As an added benefit the transformation cycle diagrams are used to communicate direction and progress to all the employees. This process goes back to anything you have read regarding change management 101, it creates a mechanism allowing the leaders to be in the driver's seat of their digital transformation. Odds are, as you stay within the digital reputation quadrant of the Lush's hierarchy, your transformation cycles will be occupied mostly by valuable applications actual names. As you will discover when we discuss contextual computing, your transformation cycle will evolve from showing valuable applications to displaying transformation elements (business scenarios). The transformation cycle is made up of the following components:

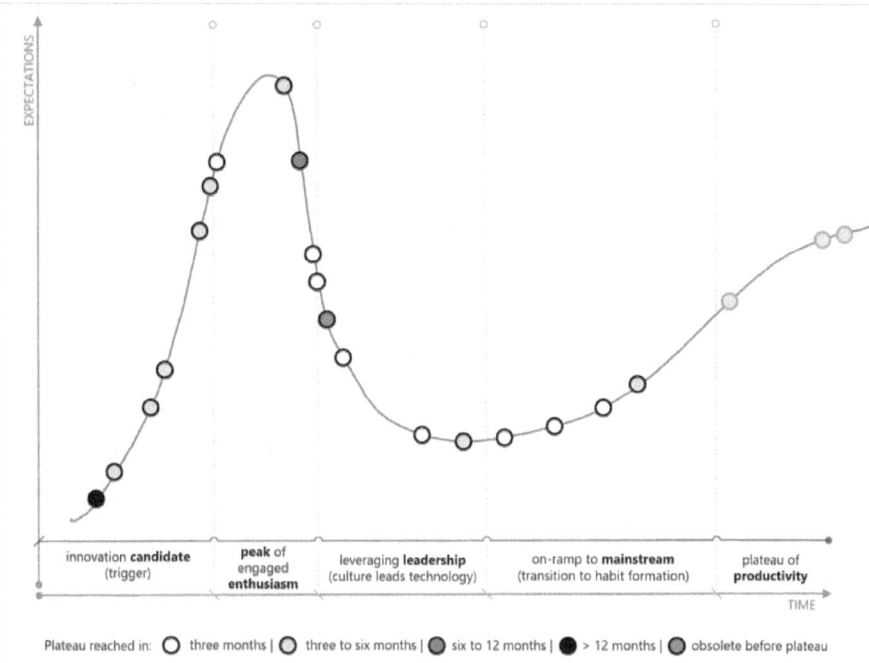

Start with an X-Y axis diagram, where the X axis represents time and the Y axis represents expectations.

From left to right place five sections and one line of colors;

1. innovation **candidate** (trigger): this is where additional items are added to the transformation cycle diagram.

2. peak of **engaged enthusiasm**: during your adoption cycle this will be the highest energy point, unfortunately as you can see the time which you will spend in this cycle will be the shortest

3. leveraging **leadership**: I like to think of this as the first step in the trough of disillusionment. This is the point in the transformation cycle where your culture will lead the technology, not vice versa

4. on-ramp to **mainstream**: designed to make you think of an on-ramp to a freeway it's time to kick it into gear as you begin to transition your community to form digital habits based on the solutions that you are driving through the transformation cycle.

5. plateau of **productivity**: congratulations, if you are here you obviously cleared the trough of disillusionment, the combination of leveraging leadership and on-ramp to mainstream. You should be proud as you have taken a valuable application or element and made an indelible mark on your organization. Be careful not to set your expectations too high as there is a stark difference between the time required to deploy and that to drive full adoption

6. **colors** at the bottom of the chart: when you meet with the organization's leadership at some frequency (preferably more than once per quarter), that team will commit to you their timeline to move the transformation cycle circle across to the plateau of productivity. Sometimes the circle will move forward and sometimes will move backwards, either way the important aspect is the local leadership is driving the bus.

The Art of Creating Digital Dependencies

The most challenging part of making it through the adoption cycle of a new digital tool is pushing through the trough of disillusionment. Creating the proper digital dependencies, in the right order, is hyper-critical for you to achieve the goal of goal of attaining an outstanding digital reputation. Our objective is to select one or two areas within the business which we can apply one of the valuable applications. To pull this off, the applications chosen must touch many parts of the business and the processes should be considered as compulsory. Here are some things to consider:

1. Finding that one or two **critical business processes** which can naturally tie to one of your valuable applications is easier than it sounds. If you are not already familiar with the details of your business, then partner with somebody who is within your organization.

2. Think about the user's **current habits**, your suggested first application needs to be close to the spirit of their existing process. Straying too far will force the user to think about things completely different, and while that is not always a bad thing, the first hiccup they experience will find them quickly using their old ways

3. Your suggestion should **simplify their lives**. Please don't misinterpret this and make the activity faster. It is hard to gauge the efficiency gains until after the individual has fully resolved, and used for a period of time, the new digital process. Without question, your designs should always focus on simplification.

4. Answer this question: What does every person need? For instance, in the service business people need to get purchase order numbers, or on the sales side of the equation they require quote numbers. Introducing these very narrow opportunities to your community will **raise their comfort level** by accessing the new environments daily, increasing their confidence.

Let's not forget that adoption is 80 percent resolve. It will be important that you baseline the starting point and set goals for you to reach directly related to adoption. Please do not let your head get too big as the adoption numbers will rise quickly if you have adequately chosen a good digital dependency. Please remember that we are trying to build a solid digital reputation. Make sure that you share the good news of the adoption to the users and the leadership in a tasteful and non-boastful manner. Of course, you yourself are also prone to bringing back old habits. Let's use the example of notifying people regarding their progress towards adoption goals. For example, four weeks have gone by since you first deployed your two digital dependencies. So far so good, you had a few hiccups at the beginning but all in all things seem to be running quite smoothly. It's time to let others share in the good news, what do you do?

1. Send an email to the leadership team advising them of the adoption metrics?

2. Use a collaborative news object from within the cloud platforms valuable applications.

3. Create the news object, and its appropriate notifications from within the cloud platform, yet also send a courtesy link via email to the leadership team.

Which would you choose consciously? Most likely, since you are reading this book, your choice will be item number three. Let me share with you, from personal experience, that at the beginning you will choose number one. If you come from the IT side, and not generally from the business, odds are you will choose item number two. The correct answer will be your conscious decision to select item number three. One of the worst things you can do is make the new platform appear as a burden or even worse an area of embarrassment for the leadership team. Depending upon the individuals they may or may not come to you for assistance in accessing the recently released news object. It is critical that we keep our eye on the ball and always remember why this first step is so important, we are building a digital reputation which is made up of trust. Don't permit your ego or unrealistic expectations of the users to get you going down the wrong path.

Digital Reputation
Make it Personal

We must once again visit the legacy of software deployment within organizations over the last couple of decades. With a keen focus on transactional systems, practitioners learned how to adapt their habits into the constraints of the software system. It really wasn't until *valuable* applications came into the mix in the last few years that this position has been questioned. Now, more than ever, we need to look at it through a different lens if we are to achieve success in building our digital reputations. Although maybe a bit unusual for some here are some suggestions to get you started on making your adoption practices personal:

- **lead by example** | as with many things and articulated in the section "driving the bus", a community, each in their own way, must demonstrate consistent use of the new *valuable* applications. As everyone learns at their own pace it is not important the level of competency demonstrated, instead positive signals that the transformation is important to everyone

- **digital coaching** | often, with modern digital tools, adoption is not the core functionality of the software. Instead how to connect these tools with individuals daily work habits drive a change in behavior. Digital coaching starts with a discussion, followed by suggested tools to leverage. We remove the challenge for user to correlate their needs to functions within often unknown and/or complex toolsets. As the tools deliver immediate value they are commonly expanded by the individual or the team.

  - typical uses:
    - individual or team often utters "if I could only" ...
    - progressive users with the desire to be more productive
    - output from business improvement or ideation meetings

- o value:
  - personalizes adoption
  - immediate increase in personal and team productivity
  - builds user confidence
- **from apps to outcomes** | it is simply amazing to watch the transition as individual's dependency on the "I believe button" falls off. The efforts put forth within your organization, in some cases for months and months, building and fortifying your digital reputation have paid off in spades. You will know that you've arrived and are ready for the next phase of the hierarchy of digital transformation when your transformation cycles stop naming applications and began listing transformation elements. Instead of your practitioners feeling the burden of determining which valuable application in the cloud platform will serve them best they are now thinking about how these tools can help them reach their digital potential.

For me, and why you see the greatest amount of detail within the digital reputation section, is the realization that without a good digital reputation you will never achieve adoption. For those of you scoffing at that statement, true business transformation through these wonderful, value packed applications, will always be just out of your reach.

Congratulations for clearing the first chapter, digital reputation. Now on to Contextual Computing, where things get very REAL

Chapter Two
The call for Contextual Computing

Would you describe yourself as a digital survivor? You know, the world has forced you to utilize digital tools such as email and file storage in the cloud. Often you wonder about how things could be better; however, you cannot seem to put your finger on the best approach. Instead, day after day you wrestle with a seemingly bottomless email inbox and a daunting business portal where you are expected to logically store digital collateral.

Long gone are those days when IT set up my computer and pointed me to a shared server drive. Between my brilliantly organized email folders, and the tree of folders on the shared drive, I was good…. Or was I? While I could locate items quickly, most of the time, requests from co-workers continued to rise as the information age seemed to bottleneck on each of us, those "in the know" comfortable on our individual data islands. Is it possible that the hope of personal and corporate "modern computing" have simply choked us in digital exhaust? Information traveling towards us at the speed of light without any context leaving us frustrated and defeated. We must think differently about how we leverage information in the future, if we have any chance of jumping off the hamster wheel.

Think about a typical day for a moment, the routines that you go through from when you wake up in the morning to when you finish your day. It is likely that many parts of your digital life are already thinking in a contextual manner. For many of you a strong association between context and applications will exist. What is the traffic like; check the traffic application. How is the weather; pull up the weather.

Now, let's consider an email which may have just arrived in your inbox. This email is from Joe Smith with Smart Computing inquiring about how the job is going at 123 Main Street. Immediately you respond to Joe with whatever information you have rattling around between your ears. Now, you have the best intentions in mind; however, since you have not embraced contextual computing, your perspective is extremely limited. Come to find out that the rest of your team are proficient practitioners of contextual computing and have a collaborative group showing all pertinent information about Joe and the Smart Computing organization. One of the service providers at Joe's site has inadvertently flooded two floors of the building. Joe's question "how is the job going" was asking about the flood, your assumption was the context of his question was about the new equipment installation. If your objective is to prove how disconnected you are with your customers and their concerns, then you NAILED it...

Unfortunately, this scenario happens all the time. You may not see it directly, yet the ramifications will eventually be felt as the customers trust wains and your hopes of bringing order to this entropy seem to get further away. All it takes is an approach which helps you see that organizing your content in context can be as straightforward as one foot in front of the other. The following sections within this chapter will explore mechanisms which you may employ today to help you master the next phase of your digital evolution; contextual computing. You are in the cat-birds seat with a strong reputation your community will happily travel with you on this next step of the hierarchy of digital transformation.

Contextual computing
The Craft of creating Digital Value

With each passing year of the digital age, we ironically get further away from the significance of technology. Hey, fact is that transactional systems will always be in play, however, it is with the "valuable applications' where the last mile of value exists. If you are interested in a truly digital enterprise, you must go WAY past those, frankly boring, transactional systems (finance, operations, email, file storage). Are you nodding your head? In order to transition your organization to this next step of digital adoption you must think outside of the box. It is not for everyone, no shame, achieving the first step of digital transformation is quite an accomplishment. For those of you, who just know work could be executed more efficiently, are frustrated that the value you have extracted from the cloud is just barely more than you had ten years ago, read on as contextual computing is your next step of the digital continuum.

The first, and for many the most difficult step, is to stop thinking about digital change in the context of software applications. Nobody gives a crap, what they really care about is their employees, clients, and businesses. Start your conversations about business aspirations or challenges. Consider framing your discussions in terms of what needs to "be done", the "pains" and "gains" expected. Once you have framed the business context, align what you can provide via products or services. Clearly articulate what you will do to offer "pain relievers" and "gain creators". Your background will determine the level of complexity with this exercise, technologists may struggle the most. However, you do not, and should not, do this alone. You may consider creating the first one with you and your team for a client group. Once you have a practical example, extend this exercise as a working meeting with your clients (internal or external). Contained at the bottom of this section you will see an example for a business owner with the desire to improve, the example is high level.

To get your head in the right space, repeat these five times before your session: "listen, listen, listen and get a clear understanding of why". Do not bite on the temptation to show the client an application which would solve their problems during this session, leave your white horse back at the office. The customer does not need to be saved, instead their words need to be translated into pragmatic solutions, which in many cases will be digitally driven. Your main purpose is to help the client. As you delve into the value proposition exercise, these tips will help you stay on track:

- Center of the right wheel | who is the intended audience, this is absolutely your first step

- To be done | for me this is step 1a, although you may start at any place on the diagram. Keep your words direct and to the point. Taking too narrow of an approach will make it very hard to complete the other sections, and too high level will make it tough for readers to derive action from your statement. The example, is for a transformation services business, communicating the business case, yet a bit high level to drive action and subsequent change.

- Pains | consider a few things; the pains section must communicate that you "get it", leave enough latitude to adjust to the client's needs, and resonate with executive leadership. If you get too deep you will run out of solutions and narrow the path so tightly that the readers may not be able to get the big picture.

- Gains | while this is not the end of your value proposition, I like to think about the right side as identifying the problem while the left side is all about the solution. Before moving to the left side, you must make certain that you have clearly identified the problem or opportunity. Socialize and adjust as required, the left side is simply responding to the right side...

- Pain relievers | armed with clearly identified pains, how will you fix it? Often, I will jump to the products and services first and then complete the pain relievers and gain creators. However, this is not always the case, you will need to experiment. Regardless of which happens first, the pain relievers should address the items in the wheel to the right.

- Gain creators | you are on the home stretch and need to connect all the pieces. Keep in mind that some will only read a few of the boxes, this is always on that list. These gain creators will be leaning into your final section, products and services

- Products and services | this is a hard section to complete as transformation is a movement and not products. However, you do not want to sound aloof either. Once you are complete, and you read the first and last box, does it make sense?

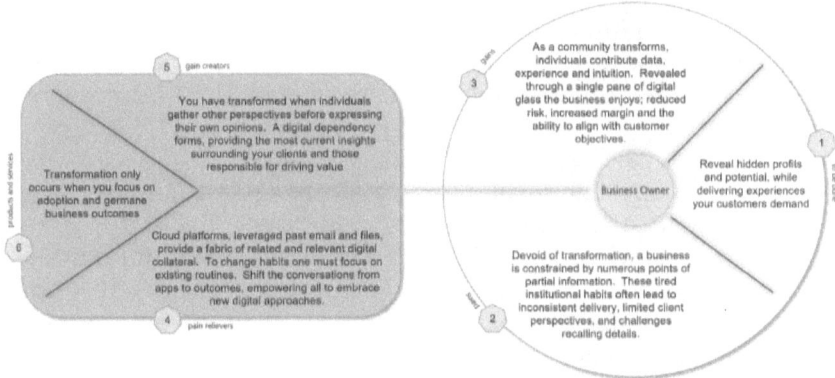

So often these value propositions are bypassed, fact is they are hard if your goal is to capture the customers true value from digital tools. For me it takes multiple iterations after reviewing, it with as many and diverse individuals as possible. You must ask yourself, are you deploying applications or helping your clients become a transformed digital enterprise?

Rethinking your data

A beautiful fall late morning in Southern California has my family contemplating an afternoon at the beach, just 20 miles away as the crow flies. As I ponder the idea, I remember that the Santa Ana winds blow strong in the fall (from the inland areas to the Pacific), it could be warmer, windier and even a bit smoggy. Quickly I move to the calendar, seeing as it is a Sunday on a holiday weekend the traffic will be tough, not to mention the parking. Of course, now I needed to weigh the overall feelings of my family; my daughter not a fan of the sun, my wife would go to the beach anytime regardless of conditions. Finally, my red Dixie cup may not go by unnoticed as with non-holiday weekends, additional law enforcement officers are likely to be present at the beach areas.

In a matter of seconds my brain assessed numerous points of information to come to an informed decision, consuming subjective and objective data points. The human brain is an impressive and contextual data factory. Let's break this down into a high-level data acquisition exercise taking advantage of modern approaches to data:

- Weather service, with location services

- Traffic service, with location services, route, and travel preferences

- Calendar, with a micro service connection to US holidays

- Police presence, pulling data from social feeds attempting to establish a probability

- Empathy and feelings, a uniquely human computing function

Our context was simple, an afternoon at the beach. Thus, all the data points are seen from that perspective, an exercise much easier said than done. Without a clear understanding of the objective, it will be impossible to gather the right amount of data points, and more importantly the inputs which have the greatest impact on one another.

For all the brain's power, the flow of data can be a bit tricky. Four of the five citations were processed in the rational side of the brain. However, your brain first processes the information through the feeling's sides of the brain, BEFORE traveling to the right side of the brain. Now, depending upon the information being crunched, the situation, your personality type, and inputs from other parts of your body, decisions may stall or shoot through the left side of the brain. This is where is gets dicey, in order to contextually maximize the value of your data, you must have a crystal-clear understanding of the objective. In most cases you will need to have access to a team of experts, some of the roles may include; data scientist, data modeler, networking and storage, security and authentication, graphing (modern integrations), code developers, visualization designers, anthropologists, business owners and practitioners. Not always the case; however, rule of thumb dictates that the more human inputs you can wrangle the greater your perspective.

Our world is overflowing with data, most of it out of context. Yet, at the cost of storage, strategies should be put in place to grab as much data as you possibly can from numerous sources, structured, unstructured, pulled from your enterprise and from third party sources. While the statistic seems to hover around 97% of data is never used, keeping that data for a rainy day, when you are looking for deeper perspective will be worth its weight in gold. Consider for a moment the gigabytes per hour of data from a Rolls Royce jet engine from Los Angeles to Tokyo. You can bet that this information is sliced, diced and pumped into algorithms and transactional systems. The trick is to make sure that you have chosen tools which can perform some fundamental actions:

- analyze the streaming data while being gathered

- data lakes for storing mass amounts of data not used today

- edge devices capable of local processing to manage data costs

- encrypted transaction level mechanisms to the edge and from the edge to the device

Rethinking your data has some of the tensions found with other enterprise environments, what is the best time to rebuild, expand, or pivot from your existing approaches to modern data management practices? Regardless of tool sophistication or age, the assessment must start with a multi-year plan on how this data impacts the business. If the data, you are collecting cannot lead to some form of action then I recommend you find another hobby. Producing a color filled dashboard with all sorts of arrows, pies, and graphs may be nice eye-candy but what does it all mean? As future decision makers enter the workplace, with their digital-savvy backgrounds and life experiences often fed by others young perspectives on the meaning of data, your data outputs will need to provide clear action.

All too frequently I find myself in a cold sweat when I think about the future of decision making. Odds are you played the game of operator as a child, the first person whispers a phrase into another ear, that person whispers into the third persons ear, and so on. The last person shares the phrase with the group and almost without fail, it is completely different than the phrase that started the game. Now, imagine data, processed in "black box" algorithms spitting out assumptions about the true meaning of the information, watered down by limited perspective. Put the cherry on top and all this kind of accurate data feeding the opinions of our future leaders. Digital savvy sure, with much of their experiences consumed by the outputs of other data elements, feeling a little uncomfortable? Rethink your data, your company's future depends on it.

Apps to Outcomes

The implementation of cloud platforms in recent years has become, well a bit pedestrian. Now, the challenge seems to be in experimenting with different approaches to get folks to recognize the value. For many years we have been driving the use of applications. An application-based approach worked, the financial model for software manufacturers and the licensing clarity for businesses was effective. It all started with the box of software, floppies, CDs, and even DVDs. Nobody had any question which app did what, it was crystal clear that Word assembled sentences and Excel crunched numbers. This concept of applications extended into the workplace as well. Remember back when your company decided to deploy a new accounting system, not a problem. Heck, for good measure let's throw in an inventory and PO system. Still not a problem until someone started to talk about integration, or heaven forbid the deployment of a one-size-fits-all Enterprise Resource Planning (ERP) system. Suddenly this idea of an abstraction layer between our comfortable applications created confusion and anxiety. When mobile devices started to hit the market and gain momentum, what did we see, you got it, a sea of applications. So many applications and so little value; however, the race to win the mobile consumer and business would be won by the software company with the broadest set of applications.

Much different than today, when one could argue that applications are simply a collection of micro-services bundled together, especially if you are leveraging cloud platforms. All these services stitched together using the newest form of dynamic integration known as graphing. Set the book down for a minute, open your computer, launch Outlook and compose an email. Heck, send me an email with feedback to greglush@lastmileworkersolutions.com. Now, when you are composing your message notice the rich text features (bold, italic, formatting, etc.), the ability to drop in a picture or render a small sketch. Yep, you guessed it, these are all micro-services found in Microsoft Word, split up into little functional components leveraged across the Microsoft suite of products, in this example they surface in Outlook. You can see similar logic within many software manufacturers tools, one that comes to mind is the brilliant progress made by Adobe and their Creative Cloud, wow. This behavior is not exclusive to the software giants, you can see, at varying degrees of sophistication, these tools across most cloud providers products. When the graphing term was introduced a couple of years ago, I thought, now that is a silly name. Yet, much like the seemingly chaotic genius of cloud platforms, it makes perfect sense when you consider that literally every feature of any given application may be graphed to one another, brilliant.

Enough of the quasi-technical background, are you ready to change the way that you think about computing? If your brain just jumped to thoughts of which email client to use, then we are not on the same page. Come on man, think past email and file storage in the cloud, if that is your only destination than I only have one thing to say; shame, shame. Talk about a great sales job... "Mr./Mrs. Customer, let me move you into the future, we will move your email and files into the cloud. You may proclaim to your clients how forward thinking you are, phooey." Before I jump off my soapbox let me get this straight, you moved from a networked solution, to a cloud network riddled with variables and latency, and decided to keep business as usual? Have I offended you just a tad? Great, now we are ready to start discussing the solution to this comfortable yet totally absurd stalling point of email and files to the cloud. As mentioned, we MUST change the way that we think about computing, specifically the transition from apps to outcomes is paramount.

It is a rare event when an organization contemplates an investment and does not discuss the desired outcomes, I get it. Yet, what if you turned the conversation around and started with "what" you are trying to achieve? Staying with the modern approaches from above, take the outcomes to micro-outcomes, small changes within the business which can collectively have significant impact. While this makes sense to many, it is much easier said than done. Context seems to be the biggest challenge when asking the question, how are things going? Subconsciously humans will adjust their responses in conversation to align with common points of understanding between all parties. Thus, when a technologist initiates a business conversation, folks often respond in terms of applications or software, this will simply not work. Instead you must encourage discussion surrounding "why" things are happening, good and bad, inside of the business. In my experience, this is a tough approach as our memory recalls only the latest details. When things are bumpy a discussion about extracting the value of a cloud platform will be deferred. All is working well, our immediate memory says, "we are good" and change is also re-prioritized. The key is to extend past the recent memories to value packed areas within the business, untapped veins of gold, mined easily with a deliberate use of modern digital tools.

In order to transform an organization, where we change institutional habits, a new set of tools must be used. My recent experience suggests that starting with relevant "best practices" or what some refer to as accelerators offer the most comfort. The best practices may be as simple as; sign off approval, or modern meetings. Each best practice, which I refer to as a transformation element, align to high level business groupings; business performance, sales, workforce, margin, and industrial IoT. Certainly, your business categories would be focused on your business and the transformation elements would capture your micro-outcomes. Over time I learned that the number of elements could be a bit overwhelming and do not show expected outcomes before and after the transformation. Thus, a level above the elements was created, I lovingly refer to as transformation triggers (suggesting action). Triggers are based on business conditions such as control field spending, project delivery, sales not selling value, etc. Transformation elements are bundled within triggers helping folks see the magnitude of effort required to alter an existing business condition or challenge. Depending upon the organization, they will be more comfortable starting with triggers or elements, either works. Your goal is to have a conversation which extends past our short-term memory.

The trick is to have a different discussion, focused on changing the way that we compute. Driving outcomes, and more specifically micro-outcomes, is the only path to helping your clients find hidden profits and undiscovered efficiencies. Remember, everyone can provide what and how, those ready to transform will always start with "why".

Chapter Three
Insights

Congratulations for hitting this impressive spot on your digital transformation journey. Getting any business to turn the corner and embrace the first stages; digital trust and contextual computing, is an accomplishment indeed. Now, before reading about the final two stages of the digital transformation hierarchy, you should spend time to get a real pulse of your organization. It is possible that the first two stages are plenty, remember that the juice must be worth the squeeze. Up until this point you had to invest significant time, yet in many cases you already owned the software (for example the Office 365 suite), and the need to seek outside consultants was minimal.

As with the other stages, I will work you in slowly with a pragmatic approach to value extraction. Now that trust and context are filling our barrels with dry powder it is time to leverage the investment and pull out some insights. A couple of computing phenomena continue to stump me. One of those phenomenon's has to do with search. As you will discover in the next section of this book, I believe that two types of users exist, scrollers and searchers. It is uncanny, when an employee walks through your business doors or launches a corporate portal, they seem to forget how to search for content. Enjoy the section on searching as insight is squeezed out when we see additional content as the result of our digital inquiries.

We don't stop with searching, although strong in delivering insight about your content and the companies' content, three additional sections delve deeper into extracting insights and value from your digital investments. Pinpointing software strengths gets us into the second section discussing the importance of understanding the primary objective of transactional and valuable software. Insights often lead to a different perspective and always unearth previously undiscovered opportunity. Data visualizations, trends and how the information correlates to your business will be the purpose of the third section of Chapter three. Talking specifically about disciplines to be considered when thinking about common data environments, points of integration, and native graphing services readily available within modern software. Finally, our last section of the chapter, gets into how intuition is blended with insights to deliver different ways to think about your clients, projects and internal departments. Natural language processing as exposed through BOTs is a great way to answer questions and direct folks to relevant information across your enterprise.

The fruits of your labor will be rewarded as you head into the third stage of Lush's Hierarchy of Digital Transformation; Insights.

Finding digital Collateral

My day started in the normal manner, start my computer, go get a cup of coffee, come back to the Windows 3.1 boot screen, enter my credentials and make a lap around the office spreading my morning cheer. The final leg of my journey would be to connect to our local file server and begin my work. However, today was special, I have been asked to explore the internet. Some of our competitors had been using the Internet for a few years now, my organization was, let's say conservative. Waiting for me was a nice US Robotics modem, a phone line, connected exclusively to my computer. As the modem attempted to connect the internet to my PC it seemed as if it was teasing me with its odd melody. The suspense was over when I finally connected and greeted with a single rectangle and a "search" button. Now, this was quite an accomplishment. I thought to myself; "can't wait to show everyone else, if I could just locate the file and folder structure, browsing the internet would be a cinch". Yet, the comfortable structure I was accustomed to for so many years was nowhere to be found. Could it be that this new Internet wanted me to just type what I was looking for? What happens if I don't really know what it is that I want? Suddenly my excitement captured earlier turned into anxiety, is it possible this damn computer and internet were going to make me feel inferior?

Ridiculous is the thought going through my brain as I typed the first paragraph. Not the story above, as that happened everyday across the world years ago, instead that organizations still suffer with the challenge employees face between scrolling and searching. Somehow, and I have yet to understand the conditions which cause this phenomenon, when folks walk through their organizations doors they seem to mysteriously forget how to search. For me, when helping companies expand their digital enterprises, I will often group users into two buckets, each having their own approach regarding transformation, they are scrollers and searchers.

- **Scrollers** | it stands to reason that workers which are accustomed to finding files on a file server or local hard drive are comfortable with scrolling. The company configures a logical folder structure and teaches their employees how to access, upload and lightly search this file management environment. Prior to the cloud, and robust search tools, this made sense; however, this practice today is like a person using an abacus instead of a calculator. Not to mention that the logic of any file structure is only understood 100% by the file/folder creator, everyone else is compromised. We are not suggesting that all folders and cloud libraries be eliminated, and one big ass file bucket be used instead. However, you should challenge yourself and your organization with one of two quick questions:

1. **Five times "why"** | popularized by every child between the ages of four and seven. Examine your file structure and ask why five times over. Each time you cannot answer why, trim the structure.

2. **Four by four** | challenge your team to think about their file structures, for any given discipline, as only four on the initial layer and no more than four deep. This exercise will force you to look at things differently.

Searchers | for those comfortable in these modern times, search may already be a subconscious activity, need something, open an internet browser, and enter what you need. However, for many, searching content is an overwhelming ask. Within an enterprise, creating a predictable behavior from search, and getting folks comfortable is key. You may consider a couple activities to help folks get proficient in searching the enterprise:

1. **Load it up** | get as much information as possible in your cloud platform BEFORE you begin promoting the power of internal search. You will not be given many chances to win over your audience, each time they come up empty handed will be strikes against your efforts and their confidence.

2. **Consistency** | although some would argue that modern search engines can search every piece of data, file name, description, and all the file's contents, you should still have a plan. For instance, if you organize your digital collateral starting with

the customer and then work into any related information, the searcher will be relieved as in their mind if they find the customer, they may have the chance to scroll through related content.

To succeed in recalling digital collateral in the enterprise you must get your associates comfortable with search. The transformation is a deliberate activity, well planned and sequenced. In my recent experience, especially with cloud platforms, they can be overwhelming for the user and I like to start with:

- **Comfort before full commitment** | let's say that you are moving from a shared file server or local file storage culture to the cloud. Ten days prior to your cutover suggest ten minutes a day for ten days prescription, like someone taking antibiotics. At the conclusion of the ten-day period, set the shared drives to a "read-only" mode, focusing on getting as much of the information as possible into the cloud platform.

- **Immersion training** | get your hands on a demo environment loaded with content and teach searching techniques within that test data set. The key is to have folks find what they are looking for immediately, show the search function (predict successful searches PRIOR to attendees arriving) and have the attendees search with success.

Invest the time in search, it may seem unnecessary at first pass seeing as we all search for content, continuously. Each minute spent with internal employees raising their comfort levels will pay off exponentially in adoption and efficiency.

Pinpointing Software Strengths

The point of value extraction from enterprise software has changed over the years. One of my earliest memories was in the mid 1990's with a fantastic software application that was designed to digitally collaborate across locations, on and off line. For many of you reading this I imagine you are thinking; who cares about the ability to shuffle between on and off line. During the late 90's in the United States, we all worked with a very slow, and immature internet, just short of having to feed it quarters in order to keep it running (time-based reference to the dimes we carried to feed pay phones).   Of course, the ability to seamlessly transition between on and off line was hyper-critical, a process mastered by Lotus Notes (Notes) and their revolutionary "replication" tools.   I was working for an Oil and Gas company in Texas and we leveraged Notes like many in the day, everything ran through this platform. Heck, Notes was the only digital tool that we used to communicate with one another, it was a collaborator dream environment. Then, a dark cloud of change rolled in towards the end of the decade, Notes introduced electronic mail to their product, this was the beginning of the end. E'mail, our first example of a transactional system, arguably the single most inefficient digital tool ever inflicted upon an organization.

During this time in our computing history it was not uncommon to have only one computer in the office. The accounting person was the first to receive digital technology, often working off a dumb terminal connected to a server located in the broom closet. Time marched on and software manufacturers seized the moment by offering monolithic solutions often referred to as ERP systems. At the core was accounting, manufacturing, supply chain, payroll, etc. Also included, most of the time as third-class citizens, would be some elementary form of file management and Email. Notes was well positioned in many organizations and at the time showed no interest in traditional ERP, so everyone seemed to get along, working side by side. However, the water began to get a bit murky as the ERP software manufacturers attempted to capture all of the organization's licenses. A strong push for several years saw organizations attempt to deploy ERP based collaboration tools, often these attempts producing lackluster results. Organizations were beginning to accept defeat and become satisfied with an accounting system, Email, and some form of file storage (typically handled on local or networked servers). Our first decade of the new millennium had nearly destroyed the collaborative movement, so brilliantly executed by Ray Ozzie and the team at Lotus Notes. The second example of a transactional system, with the monolithic ERP system, had unfortunately set the stage for stunted digital growth.

Service oriented architectures (SOA) helped lead the way to integrating products to one another. Although the ERP software manufacturers were holding on tight to their exclusive systems, we were starting to see our first move towards the possibility of leveraging best in class solutions. At the same time, the Internet and SaaS providers were busting onto the digital landscape, challenging the Enterprise to reconsider their approaches and commitments to these monolithic ERP systems. A long overdue movement was on the horizon, but the biggest question remained, would the Enterprise be able to accept these positive changes? Certainly, a level of comfort had been established leading towards the complacency by many to keep things "as-is". Unfortunately, for those suspended in yesteryear, the value of their digital investments has peaked, isolated to a small percentage of functionality in transactional systems, including accounting, service management, manufacturing systems, and Email. Ironically, the promise of the holistic ERP system is still alive and well; however, it looks totally different, now encapsulated in inclusive cloud platforms.

To take advantage of the shifting sands and fully embrace the promise of ERP, you must change your perspective. Start by separating transactional systems from digital collateral systems. The simplest way to achieve the balance between what belongs inside of transactional system, and what should reside outside, is to understand the primary purpose of your Enterprise applications. This sounds simple enough; however, we often allow non-software variables impact our decision process. For instance, let's say that you are the person responsible for collections. You are comfortable working inside of the accounting system yet understand that to be effective at your job you need to access and reference more than just a plain text field connected to the accounting AP record. Collections is all about understanding all of the related data, access to conversations and journals, even insight from your deal pipeline. Yet, you are left to make the best of it, attempting to flex the accounting system to provide collaborative content required to decrease the current 48 to 54 day average day sales outstanding metrics.

The first step is to establish and communicate the primary purpose of your Enterprise applications, be as objective as possible and summarize these objectives in three bullets or less. Next, with your newly found objective assessment of the digital tools at your disposal, start to map where information may cross over between these applications. Often, accompanying information is workflow, how will you take advantage of triggers and actions to and from these tools? This is where the effort required will vary significantly between those of you with legacy systems and those fortunate enough to have modern, cloud based digital tools.

Armed with your data relationships and workflow you are ready to lay out a deliberate plan forward which leverages the power of both the transactional systems and your digital collateral systems. It is only when you see each part as their own unique value that you will be able to put them together and create a symphony for your digital enterprise.

Undiscovered Opportunity

I have referenced this luscious quote a thousand times; "have you replaced your employees' bicycles with Ford F150s and wonder why they still only drive on bike paths?". Our past can influence current behaviors in both negative and positive ways. The so-called comfort zone, which many individuals stay within for various social-economic reasons, is weighted heavier towards the habits which do not always move us forward. Unfortunately, innovation is often curtailed when the comfort zone represents your boundaries for experimentation. What is the significance of this chatter? Undiscovered opportunity requires individuals to think about things completely different and be willing to fail along the way. A place where many institutional employees are not comfortable. It is only at the apex of the "I know it can do X" where we will unlock these undiscovered opportunities.

Let's start with a simple example from the service industry. Successful service companies will often have a blend of scheduled and unscheduled work. Scheduled work is anything which we can plan for, typically a maintenance contract or a project. Unscheduled work, on the other hand, might be comprised of service calls or other emergency activities. Understanding the patterns of your field workers will assist you in maximizing your profit by dispatching those workers closest to the job sites. For years intelligent scheduling programs had been in existence using GPS coordinates for the worker and the destination. Instead, if we look at this a little bit differently, we may seek to understand the driving patterns of the worker, the worker cost, familiarity with the job site, and relationship with the client. These variables will give us greater perspective and allow us to choose the optimum resource. In order to execute such a plan, we would need to connect to various systems and create algorithms which balance the weight of each input to obtain the optimum output. Just over the last few years this capability is now within financial reach.

Yet, as with many parts of the business, we are burdened with our own legacy. Certainly, you have heard the idiom; people, process and technology:

- **People**: if the systems that you are dealing with are older than say seven years, people will be a larger factor then you might expect. Our digital landscape is changing at record pace. Just a handful of years ago if the enterprise wanted any deviation from the provided software, it often meant customization. While often partners help build the customization, there is generally an individual, or a team of people, who have come up with a design. Often, this deep-rooted sense of ownership, which during the initial build was expressed as passion, now may become roadblocks when faced with impending change.

- **Process**: I will never forget my first corporate CIO job. The President of the organization knew that I had come from a smaller service company and he advised me to dream like never before. Initially I was a bit perplexed as I, most likely similar to you, have been passionate about what I do for many years. Yet as we discussed his comment further, we began to unpack the reality of how we think about innovation. If our budget was always $100 then our brain would be thinking of things, often as a state of compromise, to achieve our objectives and goals within the $100 budget. Essentially, we are limiting ourselves as we rationalize decisions. For many, this can be crippling to the organization and ironically to your career. You must learn to get into a head-space which allows you to see everything that is possible, and once at that place, then whittle them back.

- **Technology**: it is convenient to consider the technology components as investments made in the past are, frankly, a real bear to just abandon. So many things are tied to these decisions which often extend far past the actual technology. As a matter of fact, if technology was the only factor we considered, 99% of the systems would be replaced as they have obvious shortfalls.   Unfortunately, that is not the world where most of us live; so in order to maintain our sanity we need to keep looking towards the future. Decisions made today will have greater impact than ever before. For instance;

  - API's: choosing or allowing software companies enter your eco-system who do not have the capability to provide API's (in 2020) is just crazy.

o Common data approaches: Microsoft, and other
   software manufacturers, have provided the concept of a
   data hub within an organization. All system data, either
   from a transactional system, form, collaborative tool, or
   even email should be made accessible by other
   applications as required. Keep in mind that
   undiscovered opportunity takes the data side, UI,
   Analytics, etc. Create the hub and spoke with the
   common data environment right in the middle.

Rooting out undiscovered opportunities must become a daily
activity. If you believe that information is not a single dimension,
then each time you speak with someone about automating their
process or enhancing their digital habits, you should ask them
what else would make this perspective smarter. People are so
accustomed to thinking about things in narrow lanes you must
constantly be pushing on the outside of the box to see what else is
possible. For me, a crawl, walk, run, approach has always worked
well. Time after time I have seen people overcomplicate the ability
to extract real value from their organizations. This is the third
step of the hierarchy, so you have already obtained their trust and
have their digital habits practicing contextual computing
approaches. You will be in the perfect place to have a frank
conversation with the business owner, "if you had one thing that
could compromise your ability to hit your numbers, what would
that be?". The response will be a lot different if you leap frogged
the suggested steps from this book. Trust is KEY and your fastest
path to providing relevant, and pragmatic solutions to solve
business challenges.

Use your words

"Use your words" was often said to me growing up as a young child. Now, it is not what you think, I was a relatively good kid. My identical twin and I formed a unique language that only he and I could understand. For those moments when my brother and I were not bickering, we would communicate using these words, which compelled our parents to remind us to "use our English words". Our older sister was pretty good at interpreting, she would correlate the bundling of letters, often forming words, to our actions. Essentially, she was understanding our utterances and creating intent, not too different than the natural language processing engines we are just now starting to enjoy as part of our digital landscapes.

If you or your team are the ones tapped to introduce BOT's and Cognitive Speech services to your organization, welcome to a fantastic ride. Assuming you are reaching this section by way of succeeding at the prior sections, you should be good to go. We are finishing the "Insights" chapter with BOTs, as a stronger engine does not exist to wrap all of your enterprise data into a nice package which is accessed by simply asking a question. Do you remember years ago when you waited for the newspaper or the morning news to understand what the weather would be like today? Now, what do most of us do? Ask our digital assistants, "hey xyz, what does the weather look like today?" Did you feel a bit awkward asking a computer a question? It is interesting when I visit with folks, they seem to ask simple (and limited) questions to computers, almost like we are not very sure how the computer would like us to form the question to seek the proper response. Often we throw in words that we think the BOT will understand forming sentences that we would never verbalize to another human being. For crying out loud, stop the madness! When BOTs, and especially those more sophisticated approaches integrating natural language processing, you should be comfortable asking it a question just as you would a colleague. How the BOT is configured is critical, and your automation targets should be clearly defined and as narrow a scope as possible. Consumers of this technology are not forgiving, they will try once and if the return is not relevant, will often discount the value and may never ask the BOT a question again. Understanding that the sentence seems a bit dramatic, make sure that you have meaningful content which has been trained, repeatedly. You will only have one chance to impress! Three approaches are provided that will help you get started, they are organized by level of complexity.

1. Questions and Answers

   Who has not heard of a frequently asked questions (FAQ) list or forum? Interestingly, back in the 70's a book was written suggesting the power of contextual, per software screen assistance known as Electronic Performance Support Systems (EPSS). Crazy to think that just in recent years the FAQ or Help screens have evolved past functional, and often disconnected from business need, contextual references and guidance. Although many computer users are disenchanted with Help, and they may refuse to return, this is a great opportunity for the simplest level of computer automation with a BOT. Take those FAQ's and Help screen contents and work them into a question / answer-based BOT sequence. Add a bit more sophistication by adding natural language processing so you can encourage users to get comfortable asking questions as they would to a trusted colleague.

   Delivery of the BOT content can vary widely, text messaging, web pages, embedded within Intranets, etc. For me, if I am asking questions regarding the use of a computer it is always easier receiving that information on another digital tool. Texting responses, with specific instructions or details, seems to work very well. Recipients may then use their phones to ask questions and the computer / tablet to run through the steps or advice. Most BOT engines will connect to an inexpensive tool like Twilio or other SMS service, providing dedicated numbers in a medium that most are comfortable, texting.

2. Business Process

   "Let's not boil the ocean" is an idiom often said when enthusiasm meets the pragmatist. Those close to me would say I lean closer to the enthusiasm or dreamer role; however, do not hesitate to refer to me as a pragmatic technocrat. Much of my career, after I came in from the field, was filled with business process assessments. Heck, you need a few different skills to help an organization evolve into a digital enterprise. A passion and curiosity of available technology tools; listening and question asking skills, the ability to see the big picture, and business process mapping. Once high-level business objectives and strategies are mapped it is important to break these down to micro-process improvements. No business, at least that I have ever seen, is not in need of some type of business process engineering. I suppose two books, which you may find interesting, have influenced my perspectives for years, they are:

- The Goal [Eli Goldratt]: a book read by many in manufacturing; however, the concepts suggested applying to every business. Eli discusses and provides examples of the "theory of constraints", suggesting that you focus on and resolve one constraint, a new constraint will appear. A never-ending process of continuous improvement.

- How to measure anything [Douglas Hubbard]: fantastic book for anyone and reminds us that anything can be measured.

Deploying process modification within a business without clear objectives and points of measurement is a fool's errand. When it comes to BOT's and process automation this could not be more important. Sure, many things within a business could stand shoring up; however, which will have the greatest value on your investment? In a perfect world your first process automation target will fund future BOT and process re-engineering efforts. As a friend and former co-worker used to remind us; make informed and deliberate decisions. Prioritizing the business value and potentially choosing an area of improvement which is not that "sexy" is a reality you should be willing to accept in order to be successful. If you only hunt

39

elephants, you may starve while tripping over the rabbits.

3. Industrial IoT
    For years my work has been focused on elevating the conditions for the last mile of the field workers. One of my favorite areas of digital interest has been around taking advantage of the consumerization of equipment-based digital fingerprints. Many refer to this as IoT or the Internet of things. While the concept of IoT is not new the amount of information which we are collecting, essentially based on the affordability of the event producer, is tremendous. However, we now must make this information actionable in a meaningful and relevant way which compels a different outcome at the point of service. This interaction with the field worker is the area which has piqued my interest regarding the use of conversational bots.

    Sometimes people confuse these bots with sophisticated search algorithms, this is not the area that had any interest to me. Instead, the bot, in my mind, can be used to take advantage of and make meaningful the correlation between a multitude of transactional systems (work order, accounting, CRM, etc.).

    Transactional systems can reside either within or outside of your computing environments. One of the greatest advantages, which struck me immediately, was the ability to simply carry on a conversation with a field worker. In the background predicting and guiding the field worker through bots-based responses. Why should a field worker be concerned with what system they must enter this... or go to find that?

As you begin to explore the technology which offers this humanistic conversation-based approach, you will also realize that our possibilities are endless. Not only can we apply these bots, and their underlying algorithms and machine learning routines to field workers, but also apply it to sales, project crews, etc. Anyplace that we need to correlate and leverage transactional systems in our daily working routines. So, are the bots coming? Yes, I believe in the next few years we will see bots everywhere performing small functions and helping us consume multiple perspectives; so, we as humans can make better decisions. Are you ready?

Chapter Four
Alignment

You have already experienced change and value in applying these stages of the hierarchy of digital adoption to your businesses. Our final chapter will propel us over the finish line as we take digital trust, contextual computing, and insights stages momentum to alter our business habits. Often the word "transformation" is bandied about, who really knows what this term means? If Henry Ford asked any person in Detroit, as he was contemplating a horseless carriage what they wanted, most would have answered "a faster horse". For me, transformation occurs as we permanently alter our institutional habits to leverage the digital enterprise. We achieve this by embracing the final stage of Lush's Hierarchy of Digital Transformation, alignment.

This book was written for all types of digital evangelists and advocates, for most of you one of the four stages will be comfortable and the others will present some level of discomfort. Our first stage, digital trust, started our journey and required you to apply your emotional intelligence (EQ) over your technical skills. Generally speaking, if you are a hard-core technologist the first section on Digital Trust was awkward. The final section of alignment is also people-centric with a heavy dose of understanding the business. Technologists, who have been relegated to the data center or IT shop, and really interested in keeping the infrastructure live will find this section challenging. Conversely, those in business management roles, who shined in the "insights" stage, will also find this final stage "alignment" hard to master. Hey, we are talking about the elusive "transformation", a state of business rarely obtained.

So, what needs to happen to drive success through this final stage if nobody will be comfortable? The answer is just the point, we must align with one another. Digital transformation, a term which will likely fizzle out, is about us all rowing in the same direction. Alignment, a word which suggests teamwork, will continue to stand the test of time. Businesses have attempted to achieve alignment across their employees, clients, partners, for decades; how is this 'alignment' anything more than letters on a page? As we get older, theoretically we get wiser. Life experiences, including success and failure (critical), no matter how trivial, are all contributors.

Yet, it is more than that, and therefore alignment, and eventually transformation, has a fighting chance. The answer to this riddle you ask, Perspective. As humans we gain perspectives through experience, listening, social-economic factors; all of which eventually contribute to our perspectives. However, if we could take our perspectives, actions, approaches and merge those with others wouldn't that provide additional insight? Now, mix in trends, which in all honesty today are considered "hunches", by accessing artificial intelligence tools like algorithms, machine and deep learning, and myriad cognitive tools. Imagine the perspective you could gain, learning things that you didn't know to ask, literally obliterating the idiom "you only know what you know".

It is exciting to share with you some final stories, designed to get you thinking about how you may apply each directly to your business. Hopefully, executing these in sequence as they are all designed to work into one another. We will explore:

- Business as unusual
    - Understanding and aligning business priorities

- Our story
    - Algorithms; getting ready to share your story with a data scientist
    - Data; move past your historical references and how to handle internal and external data
    - Assumptions; seeing things differently, transitioning assumptions to action

- Speed Learning
    - Learning like never before
    - From predictions to prescriptions

Business as Unusual

Your interview went fantastic and you remain to be pleasantly surprised on how forward thinking everyone appears to be, this may be a great career fit. With the first round of meetings behind you they invite you back to "get a feel" for the company by spending a day with several future teammates.   Edgar, the accounting manager, welcomes you into his office. He is warm and inviting, and after some small talk suggests that you look at a presentation about the company. As he shuffles through the stack of folders on his desk your enthusiasm begins to wane. "Ahh, here it is" Edgar announces as he pulls the tattered paper copy of PowerPoint 1997 slides. Progressing through the slides, covered with early 2000s clipart, you tell yourself it is all okay as you look forward to meeting with Angela from Sales, certainly the front of the company must be using tools from this decade! Angela did not disappoint, we met in a small conference room with a 48" Microsoft Surface touchscreen. Standing next to the screen Angela starts the conversation, bouncing from email to email and navigating to her cloud-based file management tool DropBox, something is off. Why is it that this company, which appears to be only using Office 365, is using other file tools? My sense is an organization that has invested and mastered the ability to "talk a good story"; however, when the first layer is peeled back, they appear to be culturally stuck 20 years back. While they may be innovative on their core business, it appears that business practices take a back seat. My goal is to land on a company that has some staying power, these folks are on a fast-moving train headed to 1980, not for me...

Have I just described your organization? I suppose, if we polled folks at your company, we would get many different responses. As you are contemplating "alignment", which will lead to transformation, the habits of the company, leadership / management team, department leads, and individuals will need to be altered. Achieving transformation for an organization is not a trivial task. Contrary to popular belief, this does not have to be a top down edict. As a matter of fact, that approach will get folks to change their ways; yet, typically change will be limited to the vision of those "barking the orders". Unfortunately, this is not transformation, instead it is simply compliance. Mentioned previously, and important to say again, extracting value from your digital investments is one-part technology and nine parts people. Positioning yourself to be immersed in how the business operates will afford you the opportunity to correlate micro-processes to the available technology stack. Certainly, the idea of translating business speak to technology speak is not new. The real change is the velocity of new products, code-free digital tool configuration, heightened expectations of clients, employees and partners. So how do we look and respond to this challenge to get us closer down the path of true transformation?

- Transactional systems
  - Most business challenges today will require technology solutions. To be clear, a business challenge is not defined as upgrading an existing system, while these actions need to be addressed, they do not generally require transformation. Instead upgrades of transactional systems can be bunched into two buckets, implementation (readiness) and deployment (go-live). Although our experience is littered with these types of examples, we may have even convinced ourselves that we "drove adoption", the fact is we checked the box once the system was live and moved on to the next crisis

- Daily routines
  - The idiom "you know what you know" comes to mind when I think about folks' daily routines. If I walked up to you and asked, "Frank, how can I help you become more efficient by using your digital tools better?" His response may be "I am good, thanks for asking". Instead, I would ask, "Frank, if you think about all of the actions that you take with your computer over the course of a week, which is the most inconvenient?" By the way, this does not always work as having never been asked that question, it can be challenging to answer. A back-up position if the person seems stumped; ask them to show you what tools (digital and paper) they use through the course of the workday.

- If your organization has or is planning on deploying a cloud platform (IE: Office 365), then you are in a great spot. These holistic cloud platforms are packed with applications, many of which are bundled into the most common licenses. To solve everyday problems, you must put the effort into learning your cloud platforms technology stack and how these tools can impact your business. The combination of your keen understanding of the technology stack and connection with the business leveraging your new-found listening skills, you should be in good shape. Transformation can only occur when the seed has been planted, in most cases coached out of the business user, and methodically cultivated to become a strong and reliable part of each person's daily habits.

- Changing the "way" that you compute
  - Don't just change the computer system, change the way that people compute! Sure, I have heard it all and the excuses like "we will never get them to use the tools" and "this is a training issue" are well, a bunch of crap. Those may have had some applicability in the past, when a strong separation existed between your Enterprise software, IT, and the Business. Now the lines are way too fuzzy, who would have ever thought that a Marketing department would be tasked with leading digital change? If that is not a sign, I don't know what is, come on, smell the coffee. How does that Pink Floyd lyric go "nobody told you when to run?" Hey, knock, knock... RUN!

The next time that you lead a meeting make sure that you are using your available digital tools. For instance, in the past you may have brought in your paper notebook and #2 pencil. Instead, consider using the notebook tool (no notepad old-timer) on your computer along with a modern meeting invitation and task management application. You will be amazed how just one person, changing the way that they compute, can influence a community of people. If you are on any social platform, you know how simple it is to get a movement started, many are more comfortable following than leading. Yet someone must start, how about you?

Our Story is not easy to tell

There are those things in your work life that you just never forget. Consider yourself fortunate if you have a few to reflect on over the years. One for me is the first time I tried to explain what was in my head to a data scientist. Let's break down that sentence a bit, first "what was in my head". Not an easy process, regardless of the topic. My married readers have firsthand experience in translating their thoughts or ideas to another human being. "Talking to a data scientist" is in of itself not too much of a challenge, instead I think about it more like speaking with any person in a field of specific expertise. Depending upon the way the question or statement is formed, your message may, or may not be communicated effectively. So, you are in a tough spot. How can you take those brilliant ideas which will revolutionize your business, nay, your entire industry, and transport them to the world of artificial intelligence? Not a single week goes by that you do not run across an advertisement, colleague, or manager asking you "why aren't we using AI"? Of course, that is a very vague question, yet one that remains top of mind. Wouldn't it be great if I could just figure out a way to translate my ideas into a workable output?

If you did not leap frog to this section of the book, it is apparent that I like to tell stories. I have found that telling a story helps add dimension when required and makes it interesting. A few years ago I was searching for a tool to help with my story translation needs and ran across a wonderful book. "Design a better business" by Patrick van der Pijl, Justin Lokitz, and Lisa Kay Solomon is a fantastic approach to helping businesses with their challenges written in a creative format, you must check it out. Included with the book is access to a very handy website packed with templates. Trust me, the templates are fantastic. Find the "storytelling" template and read the tips on its use, very helpful. The example that I am going to provide will be in context of an Industrial Internet of Things (IIoT) design that we were translating to a handful of data scientists and internal supporters. Our project, which was narrowly scoped, had a total of eight "stories". I started with the business need template to collaborate with the organization and nail down what we were trying to accomplish.

Once we came to consensus, I created an outline of which stories would be relevant and support one another. It is critical that you can thread a string through all of the stories. For me, it was tough to get started, even with the tools provided by Design a Better Business. Hopefully this example, based on the IIoT project, will get you kick started:

Story: Unmanned and Unitary (highest level story)

- Subject
    - Clients with unmanned buildings, a significant density of unitary systems and a desire to transition to condition-based service and maintenance.

- Goal
    - Maximize client comfort and asset life by consuming and correlating all factors which holistically affect the building as a constantly changing environment.

- Audience
    - Our portfolio clients (with >1 building) and their customers
    - Our internal and external workforces

- Before
    - Unmanned and unitary system-based buildings often go together. While larger properties have property managers and central plants; a significant majority of unmanned buildings (94% of all buildings per a survey conducted in 2014) are less sophisticated and in many cases, may only have localized elementary control

- Set the Scene
    - The simple fact is the barrier to entry to work on unitary systems is quite low. In the small to medium business space it is not unusual to see inexperienced, untrained, and 1 to 2-man companies. Without substantial forms of differentiation, we will continue to face margin challenges in a sliding and commoditized labor market

- What's the Point?
    - To go head-to-head with our competitors, simply turning wrenches, is an exercise in futility. Instead our best approach would be to leverage our size and ability to invest in science-based approaches to field service.

- Conclusion
    - Our ability to invent, test, and tune designs across our broad customer base is unmatched in our service areas. Admittedly our concepts could be perceived as "cutting edge" and a bit risky. However, our efforts today will position us favorably for years to come with respect to margins and available labor.

- After
    - A digital convergence of data spanning site logistics, PM contract configuration, site automation, financial performance, asset probability of failure, client relationships, influencers affecting the building has a solution, and worker skills. These variables leveraged through artificial intelligence algorithms designed to enhance customer value and increase productivity. Our investments in IOT and science-based approaches will change our industry.

Years ago, a CFO I worked with told me, "Greg, the odds of me scrolling down to read content, is very low". He continued, "anyone can get their point across in 100 words, yet only the skilled communicators can explain themselves in 10 words". The folks at Design a Better Business must have also worked with our CFO, you will see that all of the story telling templates are deliberately designed with small fields for your words. It takes me days to write these stories, I take a first pass often packed with too many words. I take a break, come back and whittle down the words. Although not evidenced by this book, I typically shave off double-digit percentages of words. This is not easy; however, you will find that less is more for you, your colleagues and AI partners.

Speed Learning

As I was entering the workplace in 1981, computers were not so popular for a guy in the commercial / industrial service business. Memory, and I am talking about hard-drive space, was nothing like it is today. Remember that unconfirmed quote from Bill Gates in 1981, when the IBM personal computer was introduced, Mr. Gates supposedly said that 640Kb of memory "ought to be enough for anybody". Heck, Apple just a few years later released a cute little all in one computer (1984) named Macintosh 128k, yes signifying the amount of hard-drive space. Now, it is not uncommon to see a handheld phone with 64Gb of memory, a jump from 128,000 bytes to 67,108,864 bytes. Interestingly a solid-state drive today, at 64Gb is a fraction of the cost of a spinning hard-drive in 1981 with only 128Kb. The point is, memory is CHEAP; forget about your past practices and assumptions regarding what to save and what to get rid of, save it all! Your biggest challenge will be to sort through the noise, a digital exhaust of sorts.

Start by establishing what you will do with the data gathered. No different than other business decisions, you need to align your input, the collection of data, with your desired output, commonly visibility and / or action. Please do not be surprised if after this exercise you discover that over 90% of your information does not translate to an action, or any value, today. To illustrate let's take an air conditioning (AC) unit, just like the one that you have at your home or office. Not too long ago I was in a meeting with an AC unit manufacturer bragging about all of the data that they could obtain, over 120 different points of information. At first pass you may think, wow, that is impressive. Yet, as you peel back the business scenarios to keep the unit running trouble-free for as long as possible, a service person would tell you that only a handful of data points are required. Where does that leave us? Acquiring that information does have a connected cost, regardless of how commoditized the hard-drive storage market has become. We need to ask, transfer, process, store, and use the data in a meaningful and relevant manner. So, I am confused, gather the data or don't gather the data?

Yes, is the correct response to both questions. A flood of information will hit your environments and I encourage you to save each last byte. However, during the ingestion process tease out the data needed for the handful of relevant data points. Allow the remaining data to travel directly to a data lake, or some other inexpensive mass data storage tool. One of the many features of a data lake is we can store a TON of data for hardly any cost (seen in organizing, tagging and storage space). In order to perform this "in flight" routing of data you will need a system sophisticated enough to perform analysis while the data is in motion. The top tier software companies will all have some degree of functionality in this arena, Microsoft refers to this process as Stream Analytics. It is hard to verbalize the significance of this next step. Bear in mind that all your AI algorithms feeding machine learning and other tools will use the data set that you deliver. Sure, many AI tools can take the whole lot, yet getting the most efficient package creates tremendous processing and financial benefits. Cloud platforms charge based on several variables, including yet not limited to; processor horsepower, memory (hard), memory (computer). Design for the objective and outcome. When you follow this path, you will also put the business need ahead of the technology requirement, which leads to greater adoption and overall user satisfaction.

Now, for one of the most misunderstood topics, predictive analytics and tools. It all starts with listening and understanding your client's business. Once you understand the customer's objective (s) you need to combine that with your own business objectives. Is the reason that you are using predictive modeling is to give you an edge in the market? If that is the case than the models that you choose should be single models, possibly only looking at one element and having the right to claim, rightly so, that you are predicting an outcome. However, if you are trying to turn around or mitigate risk within your organization, you may need to look at multiple pieces of equipment and their predictive models to see how, when combined with one another, create different perspectives which may alter your course of action. These are very different approaches, they all need predictive models and data, certainly investment, but their level of sophistication is vastly different. Both are valuable, the bottom line will be how well aligned the model is to your business conditions and environment.

Learning models, and the algorithms contained within, can drive incredible value to your business. It is key that you understand how the outputs of these data science-based objects influence action within your current operating environments. Keep in mind that IIoT, data sciences, and even workforce sciences, are as much about the tools as they are about the cultural and market-based changes required to truly evolve your operation.

Epilogue
Lush's Hierarchy of Digital Transformation

The transition that we see ourselves in is significant. Sure, a few years ago we moved our on-premise or data center managed content to the cloud; however, did we really change? For many, we checked that box and said, "hey we are in the cloud, hooray". Everything seemed to be fine until one day the CFO asked, why are we spending all this money, on just E'mail and file storage? For me, and satisfy my lifelong ambition to elevate the worker, I was delighted to hear the pressure, FINALLY coming from the business, forcing change.

No doubt, this is NOT easy. The tools and habits that organizations have are indeed lackluster with respect to the Digital Enterprise. Yet, the prioritization and breadth of change initiatives to help the organization leverage their investments are just now starting to catch on. Bear in mind that the platform has been set, your ability as an organization to compete in the future is dependent upon your ability to accept and harness perpetual change. To achieve these exceptionally challenging objectives it will require strong leadership, a solid technology stack, and sheer will power.

My intentions with this book, and my previous book, is to provide some thought-provoking perspectives. However, if you need help correlating these ideas to your business do not hesitate to reach out: greglush@lastmileworkersolutions.com or via LinkedIn https://www.linkedin.com/in/greg-lush-4881734a/ . If you would like to order additional copies of this book, or my previous book on work life stories, please search for Greg Lush at lulu.com